4 STEPS
To
Healing

4 STEPS
To
Healing

"We are all angels with one wing;
when we are together, we can fly"

Dr. Robert Rapiti

To order additional copies of this book, contact:
Xlibris Corporation
0-800-644-6988
www.xlibrispublishing.co.uk
Orders@xlibrispublishing.co.uk
305457

CONTENTS

FOREWORD TO 4 STEPS
BY MR MARK KLEINSCHMIDT

I T IS WITH great pleasure and an honour to give an attestation of Dr Robert Rapiti, a medical practitioner of note with an MBA to his credit.

Dr Rapiti's website reveals that, "*He sees himself as a champion of the people trying to get a fair deal when it comes to healthcare*". This is a fact. It was his conscious decision to open his medical practice uncompromisingly in Mitchells Plain, not the "leafy suburbs" to cash in on the more affluent patients.

Dr Rapiti has purposefully avoided the jet-set mansions and practiced in Mitchells Plain for the past 30 years, where he has established himself as an "institution" and philanthropist. He avoids the spotlight and gives of his expertise and time unselfishly.

After 20years of personal encounters and experience with those suffering from substance abuse, Dr Rapiti has documented a stark and seminal account in his "4-Steps" book. Avid readers of his frequent contributions to the daily newspapers may have caught a glimpse of his material on drug abuse.

Where others have failed, Dr Rapiti has managed to capture the essence of the rehabilitation process to assist drug users and those affected by the abuse in his book. It is succinct and free of medical jargon or senseless rhetoric, yet the coherent step-by-step approach to fighting the scourge is easily digested by the reader.

Dr Rapiti's "4-Steps" is a must have for each household and I salute a 'son of the soil', so passionate about his subject with his latest offering. It is a pity that those in authority do not always heed Dr Rapiti.

MARK R.H. KLEINSCHMIDT is a former Principal, De Duine Primary School, Lotus River and an elected Mitchells Plain Role Model, featuring in the book, "Mitchells Plain—A Place in the Sun"

Testimonies from people, who benefitted from the 4 Step Program

1) I have been struggling with two addict sons for over 30 years and in that time, there wasn't a support group I hadn't gone go to. It is only when I attended the 4 Steps program I realised that I am not the user and I am not responsible for what my children do. I got back my life and I am still happily working at 70. Thanks to the 4 Steps Program.

   Maureen, Home nurse, Cape Town

2) I joined 4steps for two months and in that short time I learnt to be more assertive; it gave me confidence to be able to speak in big groups.

   Ethel Nursing sister for mentally challenged

3) The 4 Steps program changed our view towards the disease and gave us the tools to equip ourselves on how to deal with our son and his addiction. Thank you for inviting us to the support Group.

   Sheryl and Derrick.

4) Before I was introduced to the program my life was a total wreck, always fighting with my son. Today I handle things in a calm and civilised way and I get along better with my son after applying the 4steps program even though he is still on drugs.

   Florence, Cape Town

5) I have attended several groups in the past 15 years because of my son's addiction to drugs but none of them have helped me like the 4Steps program has. Today I feel more confident. I put the focus on myself and I am no longer shy to speak in public because of the program

   Sylvia, school teacher Cape Town

6) I lost my little grandson in a crossfire gang shooting about 15 years back and I have an adult son struggling with heroin. I cried every night not knowing what to do. Ever since joining the 4 steps support group about a year ago and applying its principles, I have learnt to take charge of my life and I have become confident to speak in public and give interviews on radio talk shows on drug addiction.

Carrol, community worker Cape Town

7) Ever since I joined 4 steps my life had changed. I learnt to treat addicts with compassion and understanding.

Fozia, Cape Town

Testimonies from residents of the Horizon Half way house rehabilitation centre. Cape Town

I've been involved in treatment facilities for the last 16 years. I feel the four step program is simple, practical and easy to understand. The 4 steps is a great contribution to the sobriety of those, who wish to overcome their addiction.

R. Carelse, Director of Horizons Halfway House

I've been suffering from the disease of addiction for almost 20 years and I have been to numerous treatment centres in South Africa as well as well those in South East Asia but I had little faith in support group structures because they were too complicated to comprehend. After being introduced to the four step programme by Dr E.V. Rapiti and through the grace of the Almighty, I've found a simple, effective and powerful program to allow me to be in touch with my inner self. Thanks Doc for your valuable contributions to the person I've become today.

K. Schilder (Person in Recovery)

The 4 steps program has helped me to get closer to my higher power. It also helped me to get close to my family and has helped them to understand where I am in my recovery from addiction.

Ziyaad

The 4 Steps program has made me realize that I have a disease. I have always believed that I was an outcast of society until I read the 4 Steps program. It also made me a humble person, which is important for my recovery. It uplifted my spirituality and helped me to repent for all the harm and hurt that I have caused to my loved ones, which is my family. Thank you DR Rapiti

Marwaan Brown

I have been in and out of recovery for the last 14 years of my life. I always had this perception of recovery being complicated and difficult but the 4 steps program has shown me a much simpler way to remain in recovery. Working the 4 steps has shown me that life must have a balance. I can clearly say that my journey to recovery has started. With the spiritual awakening and the 4 steps I am able to show my gratitude and appreciation to people, who have shown me the way.

Thanks

R. Mohamed

4 Steps has offered me a new way of life and to have an attitude of gratitude. To appreciate what I have and what is around me. It has brought me closer to God and to better myself; refuelling my drive and has helped me to achieve a greater quality of life. I wish to be a motivation to others; achieve my goals with direction, determination and dedication by being the best that I can be.

Dinesh Dayaan

I have not been implementing every step into my recovery yet, but the little steps that I have implemented have really changed my way of thinking about my addiction. Thanks to the 4 Steps program.

Shameegh

The 4 steps 2 recovery has given me a new perspective on recovery and drug addiction. It made me realize that recovery can be quite simple; life is simple, it's me that makes it difficult and complicated. The 4 steps 2 recovery has made me think before I talk, especially to my parents (the 2 people, who love me unconditionally and who have always been caring for me) because I've realized the hell I've put them through! As my recovery is growing I am realizing more things along the way!

Thanks Doc!!!!

Toufieka Latoe

The 4 steps 2 Recovery gave me a better understanding not only on drug addiction but also on everyday life. I found different ways to cope with difficult feelings and emotions and learnt how not only to respect myself but love myself. Through the program I have learnt how to mend relationships with my family. The way I see it, 4 steps taught me, without God in my life, nothing will come right. So the 4 steps taught me more than I had hoped for.

With Love and Respect

Reza Solomons

I have taken out only positive methods to recover with the help of the 4 steps program because I am learning to love and respect myself more than I have done before and I realise that I am the most important person for my recovery.

Waaiz Hoedemaker

DEDICATION

I would like to dedicate this booklet/Manual to all the people with addiction (PWA's) and their families, who are suffering from the pain of addiction.

INTRODUCTION

THE PRIMARY AIM of this book/manual is to help people with addiction (PWA's) and their families to cope with the vexing problem of addiction.

Working in a low income area of Mitchells Plain, Cape Town, South Africa as a general practitioner for over 30 years, I had many patients presenting to me with drug and alcohol related problems. Over the last decade the majority of the patients seeking help were teenagers and young adults. I discovered that I was totally unequipped to help my patients, who sought my help in the early years of my practice. All I could do was to treat the bruises of beaten up spouses and fill out forms for the police, mainly in my Sunday morning sessions, a task I did not enjoy as a young and new practitioner.

The seriousness of the problem only hit home when I discovered my children and my late wife were addicted to alcohol and substances. What shocked me was how easily my children turned to drugs in spite of the careful guidance I gave them about the ill-effects of substances from the tender age of 6 years because I was aware of what lay ahead of them in the streets of Cape Town, the drug Capital of the world.

When I made the startling discovery of the substance abuse in my family, I felt as though I was hit by a ton of bricks; I did not know where to turn to; what to do and how to react. I was totally lost. None of my medical training could help me. In medical school and in my hospital training all the emphasis was on the diseases of alcohol, like cirrhosis of the liver; liver failure and epilepsy. Nothing was ever mentioned about addiction and its effects on the individual's mind and his/her family. When I discovered that my family was afflicted with the disease I tried everything to stop them from their addiction but I failed all the time.

I went on searching for answers. I needed to save my family from self destruction and retain my sanity in order to function effectively at work.

My first port of call was to a psychiatrist. I remember very vividly the day I met him. I was full of expectation that he was going to prescribe the magic tablet and put me out of my misery. To my disappointment he seemed least concerned about my pain or my family's plight. He very casually mentioned that he would see what he could do and that is where it ended. I never heard from him again.

My sister suggested that I attend an Alanon meeting, a support group for families of alcoholics. I was initially skeptical because I felt that I did not need the help; my family needed it or so I thought. It was much later that I realised how much of help I too needed. I thought I had nothing to lose by attending so I went to my first meeting with some trepidation and some embarrassment. From that first meeting, I decided to attend every meeting relating to addiction. These included open AA meetings, Alanon meetings, open NA meetings and Naranon meetings. I attended these meetings with religious fevour in a desperate attempt to understand addiction as well as to save my family from this baffling problem, which was destroying all of us.

I read every self help book I could lay my hands to get more insight into this baffling disease.

It was at an AA meeting that I learnt for the first time that addiction is a disease.

I attended meetings for over ten years; ran a Naranon support group for over five years and learnt a tremendous amount about addiction at these meetings to help my patients. I became a well known speaker at schools and churches on the topic of addiction and wrote several letters to the local papers to enlighten the public and policy makers on the devastating effects of addiction.

I am pleased to say that by equipping myself with the knowledge on how to deal with addiction, I have helped many young men and women with the problem.

The origin of 4 Steps Program

One morning I remember counseling a young 17 year old heroin addict. I tried to introduce him to a simplified version of the NA's 12 steps, when he informed me with a blank look on his face that he could not read. I was dumbstruck. I could not let this young man leave without a message so I sat in front of my PC and wrote four simple steps for recovery. I later looked at these steps and discovered that it was a highly abridged and simplified version of the 12 steps.

When I attended the different support groups I noticed there were several books written on the 12 steps trying to explain the steps because the steps were so *complicated to understand, even for highly educated people. I once overheard a seventy year old retired school teacher, who attended the AA for over four years, proudly saying that she hasn't gone beyond the fourth step of the 12 steps.*

It was at this point I realised that the AA's 12 steps, which was cloned by all other support groups needed urgent revision if we are to combat the spiral of addiction especially amongst the youth, most of whom were semi-literate because they dropped out of schools at an early age due to their addiction. Many of our youth were and are languishing in our juvenile jails as repeat offenders with absolutely no future other than a life of crime, drugs and gansterism.

Out of this need to have a simple program to help PWA's, the 4-Step support group was started using the 4-step program that I wrote for the 17 year old lad, who couldn't read. The first meeting was held at a local high school, Westridge High, Mitchells Plain, Cape Town in October, 2010. The group meets weekly on a Saturday. Six other groups started in Cape Town. The aim was to set up groups through out the country, with a strong emphasis on simplicity; the least amount of rules and at no cost to people attending the meetings.

My aim was to have a support group in every suburb in the world, by translating the 4—Steps into as many languages as possible. The idea was to get everyone, regardless of their level of education to become fully acquainted with the concepts on how to deal with addiction with the least amount of academic jargon or training.

I firmly believe that drug counseling does not require sophisticated training nor should it be restricted to professionals like psychologists and social workers. I based this belief after witnessing the work done by ex-users in TC (therapeutic Communities)to counsel recovering users/residents. They seem to have a better rapport with the users than hard core professionals from the medical disciplines

Four—Steps was my way of teaching simple principles to simple people like one would teach CPR to the lay public. I do hope this booklet will achieve that goal.

*AA—Alcoholics anonymous—group for alcoholics
*Alanon—support group for families and friends of alcoholics
*NA—Narcotics Anonymous—support group for drug addicts
*Naranon-support group for families and friends of addicts

ACKNOWLEDGEMENT

THERE IS A saying that you can never truly understand another person's pain until you walk a thousand steps in his/her shoes. I need to thank my family, who were so badly afflicted by the disease of addiction. The pain of their addiction and the pain I had to endure, served as a catalyst to help me understand addiction and to make sense of its puzzling nature.

I wish to thank the many friends and acquaintances I met at the AA, Alanon, NA; and Naranon meetings, who shared their stories at meetings so openly and so willingly.

I owe a huge debt of gratitude to a great number of people for helping me put this book together; for teaching me about addiction and to my many friends in the support groups for the immense faith that they had in me to write this book and by doing so, I hope to introduce to the world a totally new concept on how to deal with addiction.

I need to thank Yvette, who had so much confidence in me when we launched our first meeting. A big thank you to members of my support group, Sylvia, Ethel, Freda, Joslyn and Maureen for being so supportive of me in the early days of the launch of our group and for running the meetings in my absence.

I wish to thank my sister Sheila for insisting that I attend an Allanon meeting, which started my journey to learning about addiction.

A special thanks to my dear friend, poet and artist, DR Mitra, from India for encouraging me to put this book together.

A special thanks to my receptionist, Natalie for being so willing to compile the books for my patients.

Finally I would like to thank my wife, Joan for always giving me the space to write my book and for encouraging me to write whenever I had the urge to do so.

WHY THE NEED FOR A SIMPLE PROGRAM

IT HAS BEEN my experience that most of our addicts are getting younger by the day; their literacy levels are extremely low and their concentration levels are severely impaired due to the long years of addiction. It was with this information in mind that I wrote this book as simply as I could.

What became evident from the stories of people, who have recovered from their addiction or remained sober for a long time was that there was no drug to stop their addiction. What helped them was a total mind set change and attitude about addiction. When they reached a point where they were sick of their addiction then stopping was not so difficult. Almost all of those who stopped their addiction, attributed their success to leading a spiritual way of life and turning to God; none of them attributed the success for their recovery to drugs or medications. Some mentioned the importance of tough love from their families, which forced them to make the turn around.

The 12 Step program used by NA; Naranon; AA programs was far too complex for these young users to follow and apply in their lives, so many of them dropped out of the meetings. Many of them informed me that they could not understand or follow the language as a reason for not attending support groups.

The 4—Step program was designed to help people, who have difficulty in reading, understanding and remembering. The program captures all the main aspects of the 12 step program but is a lot easier to remember. The program takes about one minute to read and can be repeated several times in the day. When a program is simple there is greater chance that the program will be adhered to than if it were long, difficult and convoluted.

The 4 steps focuses on the importance of spirituality in one's life; the importance of correcting the faults within one's self; the value of family and finally the importance of showing gratitude in one's life for all that one has. The program is included in this manual.

The 4—step program is so simple that it should be practiced as many times as possible in the course of the day for it to become part of one's life.

The program should be done in the morning on awaking and this should be coupled with 5 to 10 minutes of meditation in a quiet place. When you start your day right, you are setting the rest of your day to be right.

DR. ROBERT RAPITI

THE BOOK'S FORMAT

*T*HE BOOK HAS *two objectives: firstly to help PWA's (people with the disease of addiction) and their families to cope with addiction and secondly to help anyone to start a support group using the information in the book without having any formal training in the field of addiction.*

HOW TO USE THIS MANUAL/BOOK

*I*F YOU ARE a PWA or are related to one, then you should read the page "What is Addiction"; then the guidelines for the user or for the families, then read the "The addicts Plea"; "The laments of an addicts Mom"; "The message to addict and "An Addict's message to society and the "Counselor's message". These five readings should give one a good idea of the pain and suffering of both the user and the families of the users.

The supporter's and PWA's pledge should be read so that PWA's and their families can become familiar with the importance of becoming part of a support group.

Why guidelines*: Most addicts do not have the concentration span to read huge books on how to deal with the different issues relating to addiction. The guidelines are short but get the message across in a very simple way. Ideally, people with addiction and their families should make the guidelines daily reading so that the message contained in them becomes part of their daily lives.*

The simple guidelines are meant to stimulate the appetite of the reader to flesh out what is being said in the guidelines. The guidelines cover many aspects of addiction for both users and their families. It is only through repeated reading of the guidelines, will the message become evident. This manual is not to be read like a story book but as a daily reminder of the do's and don'ts to keep within the straight and narrow and to keep out of trouble.

How to set up a support group

A group should meet at a designated place and time on a regular basis. Support groups can hold meetings just about anywhere: in a home; school class room or in a religious hall. The number of people at a meeting is not as important as the commitment of those attending.

The chairperson opens the meeting with the opening prayer followed by the welcome note.

Next, members are asked to read, "what is addiction" and the two pledges.

The message in the book becomes alive when it is read out aloud.

The guidelines

Four or five guidelines are read by each member present from both sets of guidelines till all the guidelines are read. This encourages members to become familiar with the guidelines and gain confidence to speak in public. This is vital to help members to rebuild their battered self esteem. AS members read these guidelines on a regular basis they become more confident in dealing with the problem of addiction.

Some of the guidelines can be topics for discussion as well.

The guidelines should be read as often as possible. The more one reads them the more one becomes acquainted on how to deal with the various situations one is confronted with in life, not just with addiction. Regular reading of the guidelines will help the reader to make the right response to unpleasant situations in a spontaneous manner. The right response to awkward situations will eventually become second nature.

Keep it spiritual and not religious

This program is meant for everyone regardless of their religious beliefs. It is for this reason, it is advised that the names of religious leaders are mentioned as least as possible out of respect for people belonging to other religious groups at meetings. References can be made to them or the religious books but meetings should not be conducted as a religious service. The main focus of the meetings is to help PWA (people with addiction) and their families in a spiritual way using the word God in a universal sense.

Religious debates must not be entered into at these meetings as this will only break up the groups and defeat the purpose of the meetings and that is: to help PWA and their families.

4 Steps respects all religions. Schools are ideal venues because of their neutrality.

The messages and stories of addicts and their families

These messages remind us of the pain and suffering of both addicts and their families. There is a common thread amongst all addicts and their families in terms of the pain that they suffer so these messages should appeal to all those who are afflicted by the disease.

These messages, "An Addict's Plea"; "The Lament of an Addict's mom"; Message to the Addict"; "Addict's message to society" and "Counselor's message to parents" must be read at every meeting to serve as a reminder of the pain endured by both by PWA and their families. In life we must never forget where we have come from in order to appreciate where we are and where we are heading.

Reading about the pain that other's go through should serve to helps us to be more empathic to anyone suffering from or through the disease of addiction.

First Aid Round

This part of the meeting is the corner stone of healing from all the pain and suffering of addiction. Members must be given a chance to express themselves freely without the fear of being criticized. Caution must be observed when it comes to the amount of time in sharing. Members must respect others in the group by keeping their shares brief so that everyone has an opportunity to share especially if the group is large and time is short.

Group meditation

There are many ways of meditating. The booklet gives you one way of how the group should meditate. Group meditation is far better than meditating on one's own. The energy of the group has a collective effect on individuals. It is best to do it with light relaxing music in the background. Spend about 10 minutes or longer on meditation. It is a wonderful way to rest the mind and bring some soothing to the soul. Meditation is one way to communicate your innermost feelings with God because He does listen even if you can't hear Him. I believe if you know you way to God, He will find a way for you.

4 steps program

The meeting should and must be ended with the 4 Steps at all times without fail.

The 4—steps program is to help us face the journey ahead of us with all its obstacles. Doing the 4—Steps program regularly should become second nature *and a way of life. The best time to practice the 4 Steps is in the morning soon after awaking.*

Attending meetings

Meetings are a way of building lasting and fulfilling relationships for both PWA and their families. It is up to the individual to make friends by attending meetings on a regular basis.

People, who are suffering like you are, do not need any explanations as to why you are feeling a certain way neither do you have to give them explanations for your actions because they understand your plight like no-else can. People in the support group have been or are going through situations similar to yours so they understand your pain and suffering.

Meetings should serve like weekly therapy to relieve one of the daily stresses of life, not just from addiction but from the challenges of life. I attend my meetings without fail because I get so much out of them. I get a lot out of them because of the amount I gladly put into them through regular service.

Serving at a meeting is one way of giving without reward or expectation.

Making friends

Socialising when refreshments are served at the end of each meeting is a fantastic way of meeting and mixing with one another and becoming more acquainted with members in the group. It is through regular attendance, can one build lasting and fulfilling relationships. I have found that no one can understand your pain like another person who has been through what you have been through.

If you are able to build friendships at the meeting then you have help at hand when you are in a crisis. Often all one needs when one is down or in the midst of a crisis is to have a friend you can talk to.

4 STEPS MISSION STATEMENT

"To care for all those who suffer from the disease or effects of addiction in a selfless, non-judgmental and compassionate way"

ADDICTION

ADDICTION RESPECTS NO age, social class; race or gender; it treats all people equally. The harsh penalty is death, jail or insanity and there is no drug to save anyone suffering from the disease accept God and a good clean healthy lifestyle.

CRAVING

Craving is what makes it so difficult for PWA to give up their addiction. It can best be described as a bee buzzing in your ear, with a net over your head and your hands wrapped in bandage so you cannot get to it. It drives you in sane. Craving can be triggered off by people, places and things or a simple flashback in the mind to set the uncontrollable urge to use.

GUIDELINES TO RUN MEETINGS

1. OPENING PRAYER AND WELCOME
2. ANY ANNOUNCEMENTS
3. 4 *STEPS* VIEWS ON ADDICTION
4. WHAT IS ADDICTION
5. PLEDGE BY PEOPLE WITH ADDICTION
6. PLEDGE BY FAMILIES
7. READ:
    i. "HOW TO COPE WITH MY ADDICTION"
    ii. "HOW TO COPE WITH MY LOVED-ONE'S ADDICTION"

8. READ:
    a. "Addicts' Plea"
    b. Lament of an "Addict's Mom"
    c. "Message to the Addict"
    d. An Addicts message to society
    e. Counselor's message to parents

The purpose of these readings is to make both the person afflicted with the disease and his or her family to understand what each other is going through.)

9. FISRT AID ROUND
10. COMMENT/CONTRIBUTIONS FROM THE GROUP
11. MEDITATION—10 MINUTES followed by 4 Steps
   *DO THE FOUR STEPS WITH EXPLANATION FOR NEW COMERS

12. END WITH REFRESHMENTS—announce next person to chair.

DR. ROBERT RAPITI

SUGGESTED OPENING PRAYER

Dear God we humbly request your presence at our meeting.

Please bless all those present with the strength
To overcome their problem with addiction.
Lord, may those who come here today with a heavy heart,
Leave these rooms enlightened and with the faith that
You will be there with them in their
hour of need.
We place all our trust in you
For you are the only one, who can take us out of
The darkness of despair
into the light of hope and tranquility.
Amen

OPENING AND WELCOME

WELCOME TO THE (name of group . . . .) 4—STEP support group. If you are a new comer, please feel at home because we understand your pain and your suffering. This meeting is for you; no matter how much you are suffering, we understand how you are feeling. Please remember that you are amongst true friends, who can truly identify with you and will gladly help you to cope with your problem of addiction.

We gather here weekly/fortnightly/monthly to gain knowledge and wisdom through our fellow members and through the literature in a spirit of compassion, love and caring for one another in an atmosphere of complete trust and honesty. WE gather here to share our sorrows and joys in a spirit of total openness because we accept that there is no single or set way to deal with the complex problem of addiction. If you have a view, don't be shy to express it because you will neither be laughed at nor ridiculed for your views. The most difficult problems in life are solved by the simplest of solutions; the challenge is to find them. Our only guide is our conscience and God because none of us is an authority on the complex and baffling disease of addiction.

Please attend the meetings regularly in order to improve your understanding of addiction and how to cope with it. We hope by the end of this meeting you will end up loving one another enough to become eternal spiritual friends; friends you can trust and rely upon in your hour of need, just as they will rely upon you, when they are in of need you.

* In the welcome name of the group must be mentioned.

DR. ROBERT RAPITI

4-STEPS'—VIEWS ON ADDICTION

1. ADDICTION IS CURABLE AS S LONG ONE TAKES GOD IN ONE'S LIFE AND FOLLOWS GOD'S WAYS
2. DO NOT REFER TO PEOPLE AS ADDICTS BUT AS PEOPLE WITH THE DISEASE OF ADDICTION (PWA)
3. ADDICTION DOES NOT HAVE TO BE A LIFE LONG DISEASE
4. RELAPSE DOES NOT MEAN THE DISEASE IS INCURABLE BUT IT IS A FAILURE BY AN INDIVIDUAL TO ADHERE TO THE PROGRAM AND ITS TEACHINGS
5. 4—Steps DOES NOT SUBSCRIBE TO THE VIEW "ONCE AN ADDICT ALWAYS AND ADDICT"
6. THERE IS NO DRUG TO CURE ADDICTION
7. THE FOCUS IS NOT ON THE PAST BUT THE PRESENT—WHERE DO WE GO FROM HERE
8. ADDICTION IS NOT THE MAIN FOCUS OF THE MEETINGS AS MUCH AS CHANGING THE BEHVIOUR AND ATTITUDE OF BOTH THE PEOPLE WITH ADDICTION AND THEIR FAMILIES

WHAT IS ADDICTION

"It is a disease that can only be cured through God's help by leading a spiritual and moral way of life".

THE DISEASE AFFECTS different individuals differently. For some it can behave like diabetes, which needs regular medications and constant monitoring to control the disease. For others it behaves like TB, where individuals become extremely sick but after completing their long course of treatment, they never look back at their addiction. The last group is like patients with terminal cancer: no matter how much they try, they end up dying unnaturally or prematurely. The greatest difficulty is to determine which person has what type of addiction. Regardless of the type of addiction an individual suffers from, there is only one treatment and that is, GOD.

Similarities between Diabetes and addiction

DIABETES +/- medications+ right foods + regular exercise

= HEALTHY HUMAN BEING

ADDICTION + regular prayer + right choices (people, places and things)

= TOTAL SOBRIETY

If addiction is treated as a disease then like all diseases, treatment, must be followed strictly in order to control it if it can't be cured. That treatment is God; attending support groups regularly and by surrounding oneself with loving and caring people.

RESIDENT'S/PWA'S—PLEDGE

WE ARE HERE:

1) TO WIN OUR BATTLE AGAINST DRUG ADDICTION;
2) TO RESTORE OUR DIGNITY;
3) TO EARN OUR RIGHTFUL PLACE IN SOCIETY AND THE RESPECT OF OUR FELLOW MAN, BY OUR CONTRIBUTIONS TO OUR COUNTRY'S WELLBEING, THROUGH OUR HARD WORK, SINCERITY AND HONESTY.

BY DOING SO,

WE HOPE TO BECOME PART OF SOCIETY AND NOT OUTCASTS OF SOCIETY.

People often attend meetings without understanding the purpose of attending them. Meetings are not quick fixes. Meetings are a way of building lasting relationships and friendships with people, who can understand what you are going through without having to explain yourself all the time. Meetings are the spas and saunas of the troubled soul.

SUPPORTER'S PLEDGE

WE ARE HERE:

1) TO SUPPORT OUR LOVED ONES
   TO WIN THE BATTLE AGAINST ADDICTION WITH LOVE,
   COMPASSION AND UNDERSTANDING;

2) TO DEAL WITH OUR BATTERED EMOTIONS AND
3) TO BECOME PART OF THE SOLUTION AND NOT THE
   PROBLEM OF OUR LOVED ONE'S ADDICTION.

*Parents attending meetings are emotionally battered. Attending meetings is one great way of giving vent to their feelings and getting valuable advice from other members.

GUIDELEINES FOR PEOPLE WITH ADDICTION

1) I suffer from the disease of addiction which I can SURELY get rid of completely, if I learn to sincerely take God into my life, every minute of my life.

2) I am tired of my addiction, the lies, the hurt and harm that I have caused to myself and my loved ones. I need to stop in order to enjoy a life without my addiction.

3) I am tired of constantly running away from my family, the law and most of all from myself. I can no longer face the person I see in the mirror; that person is not the real me; I need to see the real me.

4) Now that I realise that it is a disease, I will no longer feel guilty or ashamed of it. What started as an innocent experiment became a disease, which I have no control over but I did not know it at the time; if I knew it I was too proud or reckless to take the good advice given to me; today I am suffering the consequences of my recklessness and I must deal with it.

5) I will no longer go on in denial hurting myself and others through my addiction.

6) My ugly actions are solely due to my addiction and my desperation to feed my addiction. It is not my parent's fault or my bad upbringing. My denial will eventually land me in jail, lead to my early death or make me insane

7) I must stop pretending that I am fine and that I can take on the world. The truth is: I have lost so much that I can no longer afford to lose any more; I no longer wish to be seen as the scum of society.

8) The journey to recovery is a tough one but its rewards are far greater than the temporary, costly false joy that my addiction gives me.

9) As I walk the journey to recovery, with the help of God, my family and friends I shall regain my self esteem and become something rather than being a useless nothing and a burden to my family and society.

10) I must stop any further destruction and become a useful contributor to society.

11) I and I alone, am responsible for my actions and my addiction; I must stop blaming parents friends and loved ones for my actions or my craving.

12) If I need to earn the trust of my family and society, I need to be honest at all times and face the consequences of my dishonesty.
13) In order to gain the respect of others, I must learn to give respect.
14) I must learn to be patient; stop with my unreasonable demands and accept whatever fate God has in store for me; I must no longer carry on as if the world revolves around me.
15) I must learn to appreciate my family, friends and loved ones for supporting me through all my years of addiction.
16) I must learn to understand when my family finds it hard to forgive me for all the harm that I caused them. I will keep my trust in God to restore my relationship with my loved ones in God's time, not my time.
17) When I truly stop my addiction, I and the people around me will see me for wonderful, caring and loving person that I am.
18) I shall commit myself to a life of truth, honesty and caring for my fellowman
19) Whenever I am faced with my craving or a difficult problem, I shall turn to God, the 4 Step program my family and my friends but never ever again to my addiction
20) If I slip, I will pick myself up and seek the help I need.
21) To prevent a slip or relapse, I shall practice the art of mediation and constantly seek God's help to protect and guide me.
22) The only way for me to make up for the damage that I have done is to help those who need my help in whatever way possible as an expression of my gratitude to God and all those who helped me in my recovery.

These guidelines must be read by users everyday to become familiar with them.

They must try and practice just one of these guidelines everyday

GUIDELINES TO HELP FAMILIES AND FRIENDS TO COPE WITH ADDICTION

1) I accept that addiction is a disease and that I am not the cause of my loved one's addiction

2) I cannot control my loved one's addiction but I will seek God's help and guidance to cope with his or her addiction

3) I will refrain from getting angry with my loved one for the ugly things that he or she says to me because I am aware that my loved-one loses all control of his or her mind under the influence of drugs.

4) I realise that my loved one is struggling with his or her addiction and whatever help I can give, I will give unconditionally.

5) I will avoid controlling or insulting my loved one but deal with him or her with compassion and caring.

6) When I find my loved one's demands or actions become too much for me to bear, I shall not hesitate to use tough love; contact a friend in the group; contact a counselor or learn to detach myself from his or her abuse by removing myself from his or her toxic influence.

7) I will learn to forgive my loved one for his or her shortcomings with unconditional love because hating and cursing him or her will only make me sick and miserable.

8) I must learn to forgive myself if I become ugly when I am provoked because I too am human and have feelings.

9) I will no longer play policeman but I will make it clear as to who is in charge by being assertive and let my loved-one know how I feel by expressing myself without fear or anger.

10) I will learn from the group how to focus on my own needs than to constantly attend to my loved one's unreasonable demands and expectations.

11) I will not let my loved one's addiction make me neglect myself, my family or interfere with my fun, dreams and ambitions.

12) Whatever decision or action I take on how to deal with my loved one will be my own, regardless of what anyone says about it. It will not stop me from taking advice and listening to as many views with an open mind.

13) I will not take any responsibility for the results of my actions if I am happy that the actions or decisions I made were done with the best of intentions.

14) I will always remain in contact with God and my many friends I have in the group to help me cope with my loved one's addiction and always try and make myself available to anyone in my new family, whenever they need me.

15) I will give as much as I can to my family in the group for I realise that through my selfless giving, I too shall receive.

16) I will practice the art of meditation to keep me calm and composed at all times.

17) When I am down, upset or angry, I shall turn to my breathing exercises, friends, go for walk and turn to God to lift my spirits.

18) I shall never criticize but give constructive advice whenever I am called upon to do so.

19) I will learn to accept God's will and let things happen in God's way and in God's time, not my way or my time.

20) I shall strive to communicate with my friends family and loved-one with love, compassion and understanding

21) I shall learn to abandon destructive negative thoughts and replace them with positive ones in order to bring peace to my soul.

22) I will let go of my self destroying guilt and ugly past to make way for a peaceful present and enjoyable future.

23) I will try new things and be willing to make mistakes to find new solutions for old problems

24) I will try and enjoy each day with gratitude as if it were my last.

25) I will learn to live with hope and with faith that my loved one will get better. I shall never give up till he or she gives up.

*Families must read these lines every day to become familiar with them. They should turn to them in a crisis

DR. ROBERT RAPITI

An Addict's Plea

Today I realise how much of suffering and pain I have caused my loved and dear ones through my addiction.
I have ruined my life, lost many valuable years and lost great opportunities.

I have made my parents; family; wife and children sit up and cry.
I have lost jobs, my business and my family.

I am alone with no money, no food, no home and no friends. It is just me, the cold night air and the hard pavement to sleep on.

Tonight, as I sit in the cold night air with my head in my hands, I want to say sorry mom, sorry dad, sorry my brothers and sisters, sorry my dear wife and hungry children.
I have failed you all and myself. I have no excuses. I can blame no one but myself for my pitiful state.

From this moment on, I want to say no to drugs because I want my dignity back; I want my sanity back; I want my family back. I long for home, a hot plate of food and a warm bed and the love of my family.

I shall turn my back to drugs from this moment on. With God's help and the support of my family, I shall conquer the evil of addiction.

I want to be me again, not someone else.

With tears in my eyes, I humbly ask all those I have hurt to please forgive me. I have suffered as much as you have in my own private way but I did not know how to tell you. I want to be home again with you.

Dr E V Rapiti 18th July 2002

*this was written at 4 am because I could not sleep from worrying about my young son who was out in the street."

The Lament of an ADDICT'S Mom

When are you coming home my son?
You tell me you are gone somewhere,
but my heart tells me you are not there.

I cannot sleep when you are not at home.
Your dad thinks I am mad to wait up for you so. He is fast asleep but I know in his heart, he worries to death about you. I cannot hide my feelings like a man can. Perhaps it is because I brought you into this world, so I understand the pain you are in.
It hurts me when you are rude and angry but my love for you is so strong, that I forgive you. I know you do not mean what you say because it is the drugs that control your mind.

Your food is in the oven everyday but you never touch it. Is my cooking so bad? Tell me what you would like? I want to hold you but you remain so far away.
You look so pale and thin. When the neighbours ask what has happened to you, I want to hide my head in shame because I haven't the heart to tell them why you look this way.

I too, am getting weary from a lack of sleep and from worrying whether you will return safe and sound.
I wept when I saw the blood stains on your shirt. Did the gangs hurt you badly? Did you cry out for your mamma? I wish I were there to protect you.

Oh my son! My dear, dear boy, can't you see what you are doing to all of us?
I too, am getting weak and thin from the depression that is setting in. I have no more strength in me. I have aged so much in such a short time. I pray for help and guidance but it seems help is so far, far away.

Son, I feel so alone. My heart bleeds with pain and sometimes out of anger. Won't you please come home to your mamma? We miss you so.

DR E V Rapiti 19th July 2002

Message to the ADDICT

YOU are special but not extra special.
You are not so special that your brothers, sisters and parents must sacrifice essentials and the small pleasures of life, just to save you.

If you do not change with the help and love you are given, then you will sink. Remember when you sink, don't take your family with you because, they are not the cause of your addiction, you are.

Also remember, in your family are important people who are loving and caring and on whom, many people like you depend upon.
If they have to die because of you, there will be no future for anyone, including you.
If you change, you can help to make the future a better, brighter and more peaceful place than it is.

DO you realise that it is not you but your demonic drug habits that are the cause of so much of misery to you, your family, and the world around you? Without the drugs, you are a beautiful person inside, waiting to come out.

All it requires is for you to realise, you are a beautiful person. When you realise that you too are beautiful, you must change and with that change, the world around you will be a better place to live in.

It is up to you to make that change. Be brave and make it.
Make it now, before it is too late.

Dr E V Rapiti 18th July 2002

An ADDICT'S MESSAGE TO SOCIETY

I know you think I enjoy drugging. That might have been the case when I started it. Now that I am deeply into it, it is no longer fun,

It is my daily curse.

I hate the way I live and what I have to go through to get my fix;

I dread going to jail or being beaten up by the merchants and gangsters or to go hungry just for my lousy 30 minute fix;

I hate the way I speak to my parents and loved ones;

I pretend that I am ungrateful or that I don't care how they feel; this is just an act I put on but deep down, I am hurting because I am in a prison I can't get out of.

When I am on my own I cry bitterly for stooping so low.

I wish I could be clean, sober and free of drugs like the rest of my family but it is so hard. I have a disease that I have little control over, and there is no drug to help me. I envy my friends, who stopped and never turned back. I keep asking God, why can't it be me but I get no answer.

I go on my knees and plead to God for His mercy and help but as soon as I am in the midst of the slightest temptation, the craving gets the better of me and I am lost to the devil.

I do not expect you to understand or forgive me because you will not understand my pain if you have never used drugs before. All I ask is for you to listen to me and the the pain that I am in.

I pray that God will be merciful and free me from this devil of addiction and return me to my loving family again; I do not want to live like this any more. You will never understand how I feel unless you have been in my shoes and I hope to God that you will never end up like me: a life full of regrets and broken dreams.

Please pray for me because I may never see you again.

Dr E V Rapiti 22nd April 2012

COUNSELLOR'S MESSAGE TO PARENTS

Thank you for asking me to help your child.

I am aware that you have high expectations about what I can do so I need to give you a reality check before you leave with false or high hopes.

I cannot cure your children. I can counsel them to give up their addiction and introduce them to programs that will keep them clean; beyond that I cannot do anymore.

It is up to your children to take my advice, follow the program and use the tools.

If your children are not interested in quitting then all the talking, teaching, shouting and preaching is not going to help.

Rehabs won't make a difference if they are not committed to giving up their addiction. Many of you will go into huge debts, just to save your child. I need to warn you that if your children are not interested in giving up their addiction then all your hard earned money will be wasted because the minute they are out, they will run out to get their first fix.

Tough love like throwing them out of the house or sending them to prison rarely stops them from using but it will give you some peace of mind because the abuse will stop; your valuables and life will be safe whilst they are away.

I know you will worry what will become of them when they are out of the house but that is only going to make you sick and won't alter the situation.

What you can do is to have faith; pray for your child; take care of yourself and the rest of your family.

Don't let them upset you because that is what they enjoy doing. Just learn to be strong and don't entertain further abuse because you do not deserve it. Attend meetings to learn how not to fall for their lies.

Don't expect miracles from me, re-habs, and prisons and from your children but you can pray for them to happen because miracles do happen.

The last thing you must do is to feel sorry for yourself, feel guilty or ask what you have done wrong. Please remember that you are not the only one with the problem; there millions like you.

When you attend enough meetings and educate yourself you will discover that having an addict in your life need not be hell if you know how to take care of yourself and deal with the situation you find yourself in.

Dr E V Rapiti 10th June 2012

A simple guide through life

Love, if you wish to be loved,

Care, if you wish to be cared for,

Trust, if you wish to be trusted

Understand, if you wish to be understood.

Listen, if you wish to be heard,

Forgive, if you wish to be forgiven.

How can you forgive, if you do not care, love, trust, listen and understand?

With forgiveness, you earn people's love, care, trust and respect.

It is love, caring, respect and understanding that make life worth living, not anger, jealousy, hate and envy.

DR E V Rapiti 20th July 2002

FIRST AID ROUND

THIS IS A very important part of the meeting. Members, especially new comers must be given a chance to express how their week was; how they feel and be allowed to express their emotions freely. This is a chance to unburden without any fear. When a member is sharing, the rest of the group is advised to listen and not comment. The person that is speaking should not be interrupted. When sharing, members should try and be brief if time is short. If someone has a burning issue then they should speak to one of the regular members at the end of the meeting.

The first aid round is commenced after the preceding pages have been read in the group.

Lines for Introductory round

1) My name is _____, (Optional _____ I suffer from the disease of addiction) my week was_____.
2) My name is (First or full names); (optional—my son/daughter spouse/ etc suffers from the disease) my week was_____.

Meditation

After the first aid round, the group goes into about 5 minutes of meditation using the method below. Ideally, soft meditation music is encouraged during meditation.

Sit upright in your chair; place your hands between your knees, bend the body down; take a deep breath through the nose and bring the body up as you breathe in; then breathe out through the nose going down. Do this for about three times.

Sit in an upright position, close the eyes gently; let the hands hang by the side; listen to the softest sounds or imagine you are seeing a rose in your mind.

Remain in this quiet position for a few minutes and very gently open your eyes.

Practice this exercise every day in a quiet place at home or work.

Exercise

Try and walk 30 minutes every day. The best time is early morning. Whilst on one's walk, the four steps should be practiced.

The 4 Steps, which follows, is recited by the group at the end of the meeting to close the meeting.

FOUR STEPS TO PEACE AND HARMONY

"Addiction can be cured with God's help by leading a spiritual and moral way of life"

DEAR GOD

1) **OUR Problem**
   Help us with the problem of addiction in our families and bring peace into our hearts,

2) **OUR Behaviour**
   Help us to change our behaviour and make us better people;
   Remove our anger, aggression and selfishness;
   Make us loving, caring, grateful, respectful and calm

3) **OUR FAMILIES**
   Forgive us for hurting the people around us;
   Bring us closer to them.

4) **Attitude of gratitude**
   We thank you for all that you do for us;
   Please watch over us and our loved ones
   As we face the challenges ahead of us;
   Help us to help those, who need our help

God will hear your prayers but you must take His advice.

Success only comes with hard work, sacrifice, determination and a belief in oneself that we are all children of God.

Our fears bring us down but our faith in God will take us up.

Let us try to keep our fears small and our faith in God big.

Dr E V Rapiti for Otto on 15th May 2007

4 STEPS TO OVERCOME MY PROBLEM OF ADDICTION

1. **My Problem**
   God help me with my addiction and bring peace into my heart and home,

2. **Me and my Behaviour**
   I. Help me to correct my behaviour and make me a better person
   II. Take away my anger, my rudeness and my selfishness
   III. Make me loving, caring, grateful, respectful and calm

3. **The People around me**
   I. Forgive me for hurting my parents, family and friends.
   II. Bring me closer to them.

4. **Attitude of gratitude, acknowledging God**
   I. Thank you for making clean
   II. I ask you to keep me clean just for today
   III. Stop me from my craving when I am depressed or bored
   IV. Help me to help my friends, who need my help

God will hear your prayers but you must take His advice.

Success only comes with hard work, sacrifice, determination and a belief in oneself that we are all children of God.

Our fears brings us down but our faith in God will take us up.

Let us try to keep our fears small and our faith in God big.

Dr E V Rapiti for Otto on 15th May 2007

The 4 Step program was written for a young Heroin user I was counseling. I read him the 12 step program and to my surprise he informed me that he did not know how to read. I decided to write a simple program for him and that is how the 4 Step program came about. Subsequently I discovered many young drug users in the prison, where I work, also have very low literacy levels. The 4 Step program has been very useful for them

The next three topics, "Requests and Demands"; "Accept and don't expect" and "Manipulation" contain useful tips for users and their families.

REQUESTS AND DEMANDS

H ERE ARE TWO amazing words, requests and demands, which are used to obtain something or a service, with completely different approaches but only one usually succeeds in achieving its goals.

I don't think it should be too hard to figure, which one succeeds most of the time. The word that succeeds is the word request. I am sure many of you have come across people, who demand a service, attention or even help even though they have no right to such demands. If you think hard enough you might find out very soon that you too are one of them or have been that way in the past.

Let us examine the difference in the two approaches and see where you fit and what effect it has had on you and your life.

When people demand something from someone, they do not expect no for an answer; they have no consideration for you and your feelings. All that matters is themselves and their needs, even if it causes you a great deal of distress. These people are very impatient and if they do not get things their way, they cause a stir and upset the entire atmosphere around them.

These people are remembered by all those, who serve them or have dealings with them as utterly rude. It is never a joy to serve such people. They end up getting the worst service and attention because people, who oblige them, hate doing anything for them.

Take someone, who is always polite and patient. They would approach you with a smile and when they ask or request, they wear a look of guilt on their face as if they are a nuisance. They are willing to accept No and even expect to be refused. Not surprisingly such people are always helped; people would go out of their way to please them because they are such a delight to serve and please. Strangely it is often these people who are entitled to what they ask for but they never present themselves this way. They are always so humble.

Do you know of any bosses, who would never dare demand from their staff but always request in such a polite manner that you find it too hard to say no to them? They will always show their gratitude as if you did them a very special favour when all you were doing is your work.

The same applies in all types of relationships including: marital, family, work or social contacts. When people place excessive demands or demand too much of a relationship then such a relationship must take a strain, which can lead to divorce or loss of a good friendship.

The next time we want something from someone, we should look at the way we go about it. Are we asking or demanding. At no stage should we ever demand anything of anybody because requesting yields the best results with a smile.

Demanding husbands, children, bosses, friends and colleagues are the most unpopular people. Nobody wants to be near them. Their attitude is so revolting that people take great delight in finding ways to avoid them.

It should be clear that if we want to get things done without becoming unpopular all we need to do is learn a little courtesy and to request in the most polite manner. Make it a pleasure for people to assist or oblige you.

Eventually the word demand should be dumped from your vocabulary and completely banished from your attitude.

Message: to demand is to be selfish, to request is to show you care and understand. Which one are you?

"Understanding addiction" DR E V Rapiti—20/11/10

DON'T JUST EXPECT, ALSO ACCEPT

MANY OF US go about in life, carrying out routine chores and sometimes difficult tasks expecting a certain result. When we undertake unusual tasks or journeys, we make a lot of preparations so that things don't go wrong. When they do go wrong, which they often do, we become terribly disappointed. Our immediate reaction when things do not turn out the way we plan them, we begin to ask ourselves all kinds of questions like: what went wrong, why did it go wrong; why didn't I think of it before or worst of all, I can't understand why things went wrong after all my planning or my sincere efforts to make sure I did everything right.

The last statement, doing everything is where we all slip up. In any situation there exists a set of unpredictables, which we have no control over.

Most of us ignore the unpredictable or the unforeseeable and assume that all will go well because in our little minds we did everything possible for things to go right.

Life is full of unpredictables. Without them, life would not be a challenge; there would be no excitement. If we do not accept the unpredictable then we can end up terribly disappointed, downhearted and depressed especially when things go horribly wrong.

The question in your mind must be: how do you accept the unpredictable.

The only way is to accept what life throws at you with grace, patience and faith that things will turn out right in the end. If we can learn to accept things when they don't go our way, we do not end up becoming disappointed and miserable.

How do we go about accepting the unpredictable? Here is one way of doing it. We can go out and do our best in life and say, "I have done my best and I shall hope for the best but if things don't work out, then I will have to accept the outcome as part of God's plan or what I planned was not for me".

When we accept life on life's terms, there is less chance of us becoming disappointed.

A good example of accepting and expecting is when parents go out of their way to help their children on drugs. When their children let them down, parents breakdown feeling very disappointed. If parents can learn to help their children without worrying too much about the outcome, they might be very pleasantly surprised when their children do make a turn for the better.

By adopting this open and accepting attitude, parents will place less stress on themselves and their children. The chances of success are much greater when we expect less of each other than when we stress each other with too much expectation.

Message: Expect with hope but also accept with reality to avoid disappointment.

DR E V Rapiti "Understanding addiction" Nov 2010

MANIPULATION

What is manipulation and why is it so important

MANIPULATION, FROM AN addict's point of view, refers to the behaviour pattern by an addict to try and get what he or she wants through devious means.

In active addiction the main purpose of manipulation is to get money to buy drugs or to defend their drugging with warped logic.

SOME OF THE METHODS USED

Lying. Addicts would lie through their teeth to convince their parents that they need money for food; a school project; to pay for an outing with the school; going out to buy take-aways; going to a movie with friends; going to church—need money for the collection box.

More sophisticated methods:

They would please parents and friends into believing that they are clean; suck up to their parents; do odd jobs around the house; praise parents; look sad about their actions; even cry that they have been behaving badly. They will laugh and joke with family. The aim of all this is to soften their loved ones and con them into believing that they are changing. Once they succeed in winning their parents' trust, they would make requests for money for things like takkies/shoes or designer clothes. Once they get the clothes or money they would thank their loved one profusely, and sell the clothes to buy drugs.

Work on weak spots of their loved ones

If parents are thrilled that their children are going to school or going to church, addicts catch up on this and they would go to school and church just to get money for their fix. They will even go to support groups just to please their parents. They will even relate what the priest said in order to convince their parents that they are sincere about going to church. Little do their parents know that their children have been high on drugs in church, school and in the support groups without anyone knowing.

Do what parents want

IF parents are keen to have their children go to college and get a good education, these children would enrol just to get pocket money for travelling and lunch. They will leave on time but never be at college. This can go on for months till they are caught out.

Below the belt tactics

Addicts would put their parents on a guilt trip. They would make their parents feel guilty about being cruel, unloving; uncaring; that their parents make more of their siblings than them; that parents are always scolding them; that they are always being put down when they are trying to come right; nobody understands them. The worst one is when they put the mother up against the father. They praise the mother as caring and the father as abusive. They would even break down and cry to get sympathy. If the mother is the softer of the two, they would go so far as breaking the marriage. They would believe if they get the hard parent out of the way, then they will have an eternal source of income for their addiction from the weaker source.

Many mothers get trapped, believing that the father is harsh and cruel and blames the dad for the child's drugging.

These addicts would go round bad mouthing their parents to everyone by behaving as absolute angels. The addicts become so good at lying and convincing that anyone would believe them that their parents are to blame for the way the addict is feeling.

USING AN UNRELATED PAST

When addicts are caught or face the law for stealing or drugging, they search for something in their past to blame for their present behaviour. An example of this is a child, who started doing Heroin from the age of seventeen for six years. He became totally abusive to his parents and family, stealing their valuables. He even went to a rehab but when he was released, he went back to his drugs. He was even thrown out of the house but he continued drugging.

When the law caught up with him and he was to be jailed for the second time, he cried and blamed his mother for not doing anything when he was sexually assaulted at age 8. Eight years later he decides he will start drugging. He kept on harping that he lost his pride, and that is why he was drugging. He even cried like a baby and made his unsuspecting mother feel terribly guilty. This child was lying and he didn't like to be told that.

Does this behaviour stop after the addict gives up drugging?

No. Addicts take a long time to change their behaviour even when they stop using drugs. They seem to derive great pleasure in conning people. It gives them a great thrill to lie and get what they want. It becomes a way of life for them

Manipulation only stops when their dishonesty and deviousness makes them feel uncomfortable. This only comes when they take GOD seriously in their lives

Why is it so important to know about manipulation?

Parents suffer when they give off themselves completely to their children in the belief that their children are changing. When these parents realise that their addict children have been taking them for a ride, they feel a sense of huge disappointment, anger and frustration. It's like putting a knife into their hearts without anaesthesia.

Unfortunately, addicts are so good at their lying that they wouldn't think twice about lying over and over again to con their unsuspecting and gullible parents.

The sad part is when addicts become sincere to make the change; parents just do not believe them after being let down so many times. The worst thing that happens is that some parents die from serious heart ailments or mental illnesses as a result of all the deception.

Addicts are convincing that they believe their own lies.

Some useful advice and tips for parents

1. Don't believe your addicts and let them know you don't.
2. Don't be surprised that they are lying
3. If you think they are lying, don't give in to them
4. Never fall for the guilt trap
5. Never allow the addict to play one parent against the other
6. Cross check requests for school items, fees.
7. Don't insist on your addict to study if they do not want to.
8. Learn to be tough

From "Understanding addiction" Dr Robert Rapiti

4 Steps Not Kidding

Our drug problem is conqueringly big
Because our solutions are as tiny as a shriveled fig;
They are way too small,
For a problem so tall.

The authorities are on a role
Claiming that they have things under control,
They are merely assuming,
Whilst parents are fuming,
Our helpless children,
Drug—merchants are dooming
And their ugly business—is only booming.

The authorities are ruggedly rigid,
Even though their policies are failingly frigid;
It is patently clear
They will not hear,
To our daily cries and deadly fear:
Our children, heartless merchants are killing
 with their deadly drugged spear.

The authorities need to face realities;
Our children cannot become ordinary fatalities,
Or be seen
as hopeless has—beens.

We can no longer allow them to be so mild,
about their countrymen's dear child.

To the authorities—we plea and urge:
 Join us to fight the scourge.
It is time to reflectingly pause
 and change course;
Your methods are failing,
Drug merchants are sailing;
While our country is ailing;

Our children,
> to prisons and the streets you are mailing.

All the hiding and chiding
Is not stopping children and their families
from hurtfully colliding.

Stop with your failing "best practice fuss",
Please come and join us:
Fight for what is right,
With all our might,
To get rid of this ugly drug blight

4 Steps is only doing, God's bidding;
By dealing with a problem that is ripe for ridding;
We must stop kidding
Cause our country's solutions are genuinely skidding;

With the right seed and right feed,
We will surely succeed,
SO to our countrymen we humbly plead:
Please support us in our worthy mission
Because it is backed by a workable vision.

Our solution is so simple,
That it will bring back the smiling dimple,
To the worried face, without feeling any disgrace.
Let's stop kidding and fiddling,
> Cause the problem, needs urgent ridding.

DR E V Rapiti Phuket, Monday 29th November, 2010 at 4.00 am.

This poem was written to highlight the indifference by governments all over the world to drug addiction, which, if left unchallenged, will lead to the end of civil society.

DR. ROBERT RAPITI

I am a street child

I am a street child
I took to the streets when my mom left me for her drunken boyfriend;
I don't know who's my dad and I don't care;
My bed is the cold pavement you walk on;
If I am lucky, I get a place under a stairway;

My family is the children on the street;
We watch out for each other,
We protect each other from people, who hate us,
And from the men in blue with their batons and guns.
We steal to feed each other;
We nurse each other when we are ill.

I am the kid with the snotty nose, dirty face and torn clothes
That stares you in your face when you are on your way to work;
I don't care about the contempt you have for me
As you walk down the road with your content suburban jive

I am only interested in stealing your phone or purse
To buy me a fix and some grub.
The fix numbs me from the cold and pain
        Of my daily life;
The food keeps my tummy from grumbling.

I can't remember yesterday and I don't care about tomorrow,
I only live for today because I don't know if I will be here tomorrow;

The police and I are not friends;
They hate us, street kids, because they can't catch us;
When they do, man it's a real shake up in the vans
And hell in the cells;
The police know how to beat us up without leaving a trace;
I cry but hold I my tears back,
Before the other inmates see me as a "moffie or queer".

In jail I get a bed, food and a hot shower,

There I meet other gangs, who want to hit, change and rape me;
So I have to use my street wise wit to protect myself.

This one time I met a doctor in prison;
He made me feel good;
For the first time, someone saw me as a human being;
He addressed me by my surname and not as some
ugly "skolly", "skelm" or "Hotty" or low life hooligan;
He prayed for me and he taught me to meditate;
It felt so good after a short session of meditation;
He told me to take God into my life,
To study and make something of my life
            And to be honest at all times;
He wished me well and shook my hands
            As we parted
I took his advice but when I went back to the street,
Drugs was all I could turn to because that is what my friends
Were busy with;
I couldn't dare stand out alone;
            It was going to be too tough on my own.

My brains were too damaged to learn anything new;
I remembered the kind doctor's words,
 but what could I do in a world where no one really cares,
     where no one really shares.

I decided when I am much bigger, I will join a gang
Get a gun and make it big, like one of my gangster heroes.

He drives a flashy car,
Lives in a fancy mansion;
Wears fancy clothes and dark glasses;
He speaks with a heavy drawl like a movie star;
He's always surrounded by
Well armed, mean looking body guards
 And a bevy of tight skirted sexy glamorous girls,
            Who jump when he snaps a finger.
He's got everything.

DR. ROBERT RAPITI

I want to be like him;
Respected, feared
And never be short of anything.

Six months later we were back in the chooks;
My friend and I were in for car-jacking;
We spotted this "larney" cruising in his luxury 4x4;
 we rushed him with guns to his head
to hand over the keys,
But he resisted
 my screams to stop my friend from shooting were too late;
he shot him dead;
I heard the man scream in agony;
We fled in different directions with our hearts pounding;
I lived in fear that whole week not knowing where to run.

The police got hold of me and my buddy,
Shoved us in a van and were held in custody as
Prime suspects for murder.

I met the good doctor once more;
He looked at me and vaguely remembered me;
The doctor was man who has seen life;
He understood why I couldn't turn my life around;
He told me it is hard to change when the world around
        you remains hard, cold and unforgiving.

He also told me, you can't change the world around you
        But you can change yourself from within.
I took his message to heart.
I have been sentenced, 15 years for murder;
I saw the doctor on a regular basis from then on.

He treated me for my sleepless nights and depression;
This time round I realised how alone I was,
I have no mom and no family;
I am out there on my own.

One day the good doc talked me out of my misery;

He told me that he too was very much alone all his life
But that did not get him down:
He treated his friends as his family.

He made me believe in my dreams
and advised me to follow them.

I decided to use my time in jail to study;
I planned to have a degree
     by the time I was released
          to look after myself,
                    and not rely on contemptuous handouts;
I was tired of being kicked, bullied and pitied anymore.

I was transferred to a prison for adults;
I saw the doctor and the kind sister for the last time;
I never saw them again but I always remembered
The good doctor's advice;
"break free from the street and earn your place in the world",
          He gently advised.
As I said goodbye, I promised to make something of myself;
Our parting was emotional as we hugged each other.

Whilst in prison I carried the message of the good doctor
To the other inmates: we need to change if want to see change
I qualified in criminal law ten years later;
I was released on parole for good behaviour.

Today, I have a good job with a group of attorney's;
I spend much of my time running a haven for street children,
and like the good doctor,
I too have become an agent of change,

As I relate my story to young helpless street children,
I see their eyes filled with hope
And my heart filled with joy.

Every child I remove from the streets

DR. ROBERT RAPITI

Means one less gangster and one less useless statistic;
It means one more human being has a chance to
        Realise his full potential;
Because I decided to use my experience
To help other street children to make the right choices
And right decisions to become better people.

Every street child I save or change
Makes my life worth living.
I believe, inside every human being
        Exists a heart of gold,
 waiting for that chance to shine.

I have saved many lives,
        So my journey in the streets
And my long stay in prison
        Was not in vain.
God, in his wisdom
  Had a huge plan for me when he took me on this
        tough but trying journey;
I am so glad I am no longer a street child anymore,
But I am equally glad for the lessons I have learnt
as a child on the street.

Today, I can never walk pass a street child with
        Any of the suburban contempt my colleagues have for him
 But with absolute compassion in my heart
because I too was down that
painful and lonely road at one time in my life,
when well clad people spat
ugly abuse on my poor aching heart.
I sincerely hope, as you read this piece,
You were not one of them;
If you were, I can only forgive you for your ignorance
and pray that you too will change,
to save another child from his misery
        and make something worthy of him
with your new found insight

of the plight of the street child that
was once like me.

Robert Rapiti 27th Dec 2009 "Understanding Addiction"

*"This poem was based on my experiences of working with juvenile
awaiting trial youth at a prison in Cape Town in 2009"*

JEWELS THAT WILL CHANGE YOUR LIFE

1. Don't just speak your mind, mind what you speak.
2. The quicker you forgive, the quicker you forget.
3. To remain unforgiving is to inflict pain upon one's self; it is slow death. It's like drinking poison without it affecting the perpetrator of your pain.
4. It's not what life throws at you that matters; it is how you deal with it that does.
5. If you can find your way to God, God will find a way out for you.
6. We are not strangers to God but we are strangers to Him and that is why we are so helpless.
7. If there is a misunderstanding, there is no reason to fight about it but every reason why we should talk about it to resolve it.
8. When it is easier to lie than to tell the truth then you have lost your soul. Without a soul, life is meaningless.
9. If you do things with your heart they will always come out right, if they don't, at least you can be happy you went about the right way of doing it.
10. To couples: sex does not make things right; it temporarily eases the pain; talking things over gives lasting relief because it touches the emotions where pain lingers and is at its worst.
11. To couples in a bumpy relationship: sex does not heal, it merely soothes like a balm; talking honestly, openly, sincerely and softly does because it deals with the heart of the problem.
12. Don't waste your time reasoning with angry people because you will be denying them the joy of destroying themselves.
13. People, who are busy working, occupied with their hobby or just relaxing and thinking are never bored or have time to complain because they are busy using their time being productive.
14. When fame bonds firmly with humility then the famous will reach for the stars with their feet on the ground.
15. As you age don't worry about the frailty of the body but be focused on the agility of the mind.
16. It is better to be beautifully happy than to be happily beautiful because beauty has a short life span unlike happiness.
17. People, who ask what they must do when they have free time, show that they do not plan their lives. Things just don't happen; you have to make them happen.

18. Adversity breaks me in the beginning but when it's over, it leaves me feeling strong.
19. God has placed good people in hell to lead the desperate masses; they cannot lead them sitting in heaven.
20. Ignorant youth are prone to hurling ugly insults; our mistake as adults is to take them seriously.
21. Only people who have been hurt can fully understand what pain is.
22. We forgive the youth for their mistakes because we too were like them in the youth of our lives and made our share of mistakes.
23. Looking for opportunities closes your eyes to what lies in front of you and inside you.
24. Successful people go beyond the boundaries of their training and calling.
25. Yesterday's mistake is today's lesson; today's lesson is tomorrow's success.
26. There is no such thing as overnight success without decades if hard work before it.
27. The wise speak less and listen more; the foolish, speak more and listen less.
28. Perseverance is to keep going on even when the odds are stacked against you.
29. Revenge is satanic satisfaction; relief is heavenly gratification; relief is achieved by letting go.
30. Knowledge not shared is knowledge wasted.
31. Be blunt to bruising insults and you will be pleased to know that the egg is not in your face
32. Many people are unhappy when they have nothing to complain about.
33. Anyone in a hurry shows they have not planned or took on too much.
34. Anyone that is permanently occupied is never bored.
35. If you can control your temper you can control your world.
36. Problems are not something to cry about but opportunities to test the brains.
37. No matter how tough the road is, rest assured it does have an end; you have to just keep going.
38. When things are quiet, use the time to silently to reflect because there is no time when you are busy.
39. Difficulties and disappointments make us stronger and wiser when we overcome them; the weak succumb to them without confronting them.
40. Live by intention not by accident; make things happen, don't wait for them to happen.
41. Great people who never achieve fame in their lifetime go on creating great things all their life because fame is the poison of creativity

DR. ROBERT RAPITI

42. The only way to disappoint people looking for a fight is to not give them one.
43. Everyone has a good and bad side to them; by focussing on their good side, living with them is so much easier.
44. You will be remembered more by the good you do than by the good you speak.
45. If all the reading in the world does not give you knowledge to make you a better person then you are either reading the wrong books or you do not know how to read.
46. If you have money and no character then you are worth nothing.
47. If your friends don't remember you, do you remember them?
48. It's not how much you give that matters but how you give that does.
49. To read and not learn is a waste of what was written and read.
50. When people let you down, don't feel disappointed because this is God's way of telling you who to rely on in the future.
51. Because our children have our blood does not give them the right to abuse us nor are they entitled to our love if they cannot respect us.
52. When people slam the door in your face they maybe expressing their anger at you but they are really displaying their lingering ugliness.
53. Friends remember you when you least expect them; you don't need to call them when you need them because they just arrive.
54. It's not how much you have done that matters but how many you have touched by what you have done that does
55. God gives us problems and He gives happiness. We never appreciate the happiness because we focus too much on our troubles and problems.
56. True friends will tell you the truth and risk their friendship to save their friend from falling into a deadly trap.
57. If you have been spending your time uplifting those around you then you have spent a life worth living.
58. If you can't save a sinking ship, don't die a martyr saving it; jump out and build another one.
59. Man has been given the gift to talk but he does not speak; the gift to hear but he does not listen; the gift to feel but he does not touch. Instead modern man shouts, ignores and fights.
60. TO say sorry won't kill but can heal so much, try it.
61. If you have a giving heart of gold, you will always receive.

A good message can do more to change the world than all the money in the world. When you have a moment spend some time reading these sayings and reflect upon them and see what effect it has on you.

From "Points to ponder" Dr Robert Rapiti Dec 2012

"Words that will change your life for the better."

CONCLUSION

I HAVE HAD GREAT pleasure in putting this manual/book together. It is not a book on drug addiction so I intentionally avoided referring to the different drugs and its effects.

My focus was on addiction and the emotional aspects revolving around addiction. I hope after using this book it will change your life; change the way you look at drug addiction and the drug user.

I have a vision and dream that the whole world will accept the 4 Step program because of its universal appeal.

DR Robert E V Rapiti
22nd April 2012